Arkansas

by Patricia K. Kummer
Capstone Press
Geography Department

Consultant:
Linda R. Pine
Director, Archives and Special Collections
University of Arkansas at Little Rock

CAPSTONE
HIGH/LOW BOOKS
an imprint of Capstone Press
Mankato, Minnesota

Capstone High/Low Books are published by Capstone Press
818 North Willow Street • Mankato, MN 56001
http://www.capstone-press.com

Library of Congress Cataloging-in-Publication Data
Kummer, Patricia K.
    Arkansas/by Patricia K. Kummer (Capstone Press Geography Department).
       p. cm.—(One nation)
    Includes bibliographical references and index.
    Summary: Gives an overview of the state of Arkansas, including its history,
    geography, people, and living conditions.
    ISBN 0-7368-0016-6
    1. Arkansas—Juvenile literature. [1. Arkansas.] I. Capstone Press. Geography
    Dept. II. Title. III. Series.
F411.3.K86 1999
976.7—dc21

                                            98-14062
                                              CIP
                                                AC

Editorial Credits
Rebecca Glaser, editor; Timothy Halldin, cover designer and illustrator;
  Sheri Gosewisch, photo researcher

Photo Credits
Arkansas Dept. of Parks and Tourism, 30; A.C. Haralson, 4 (bottom), 6, 10, 15
Dembinsky Photo Association/Terry Donelly, cover
One Mile Up, Inc., 4 (top)
Robert McCaw, 5 (top)
The Museum of Mobile, 22
Transparencies, Inc./Jane Faircloth, 18
Unicorn Stock Photos, 16, 36; Dick Keen, 5 (bottom); Doris Brookes, 8; Jay
    Foreman, 33; Dennis MacDonald, 34
UPI/Corbiss-Bettman, 27, 29
Visuals Unlimited/Mark E. Gibson, 21; Jeff Greenberg, 24

Table of Contents

Fast Facts about Arkansas

State flag

Location: In the south-central United States

Size: 53,182 square miles (137,741 square kilometers)

Population: 2,522,819 (U.S. Census Bureau, 1997 estimate)

Capital: Little Rock

Date admitted to the Union: June 15, 1836; the 25th state

Nicknames: The Land of Opportunity, The Natural State

Mockingbird

Apple blossom

Largest Cities:
Little Rock,
Fort Smith,
North Little
Rock,
Pine Bluff,
Jonesboro,
Fayetteville,
Hot Springs,
Springdale,
Jacksonville,
West Memphis

State bird: Mockingbird
State flower:
Apple blossom
State tree: Pine
State songs: "Arkansas
(You Run Deep in
Me)" by Wayland
Holyfield and "Oh,
Arkansas" by Terry
Rose and Gary Klaff

Pine

Chapter 1
Arkansas Diamonds

North America's only diamond site is in southwestern Arkansas near Murfreesboro. John Huddleston discovered diamonds on his land in 1906. He sold the land to Samuel Winston Reyburn for $36,000.

Several mining companies rented the land until 1949. They found thousands of diamonds. Manufacturers used the diamonds in jewelry. Other manufacturers used diamonds to make cutting tools.

Two people owned sections of the diamond mine from 1952 to 1972. In 1972, the state of Arkansas purchased both sections and made

North America's only diamond site is in southwestern Arkansas. People can search for diamonds there.

them into a state park. Crater of Diamonds State Park opened in 1972.

Searching for Diamonds

Today, no companies look for diamonds in Crater of Diamonds State Park. Diamonds lie near the surface. But there are not many diamonds deeper in the soil. Companies do not think there are enough diamonds to make a profit.

Crater of Diamonds State Park is the world's only diamond site that is open to the public. Visitors search for diamonds in fields. They keep any that they find.

People have found more than 70,000 diamonds at the Arkansas diamond site since 1906. The Arkansas Diamond Company found the largest diamond in 1924. It weighed 40.2 carats. One carat equals 200 milligrams (5.7 ounces). In 1990, visitor Shirley Strawn found a 3.03-carat diamond. A jeweler cut it in 1998. He found that it was a perfect diamond. Diamonds with no flaws are very rare.

The Natural State

The Natural State is one of Arkansas' nicknames. People gave it this name because of the state's

Water from Mammoth Spring forms the Spring River.

outdoor beauty. The Ozark National Forest and Ouachita (WOSH-i-taw) National Forest cover much of western Arkansas.

Arkansas also has famous springs. Hot Springs National Park is known for its 47 springs of hot water. People can bathe in some of them. At Mammoth Spring, almost 10 million gallons (38 million liters) of water flow to the surface each hour. The water forms Spring River.

Chapter 2
The Land

Arkansas is in the south-central United States. Six other states border Arkansas. Missouri lies to the north. Tennessee and Mississippi are Arkansas' eastern neighbors. Louisiana lies to the south. Oklahoma and a small part of Texas border western Arkansas.

Three rivers form parts of Arkansas' borders. The St. Francis River flows between Missouri and Arkansas. The Mississippi River divides Arkansas from Tennessee and Mississippi. The Red River lies between Arkansas and Texas.

Lake Chicot is near the Mississippi River in southeastern Arkansas. Lake Chicot is the largest natural lake in Arkansas. It is an oxbow

The Mississippi River divides Arkansas from Tennessee.

lake. An oxbow lake is a U-shaped lake formed when a river changes course.

Arkansas' Plains

The Mississippi Alluvial Plain covers about one-third of eastern Arkansas. Flooding from the Mississippi River created this area of rich soil.

The Mississippi Alluvial Plain has two main parts. The eastern alluvial plain is the Delta. The Mississippi, St. Francis, and White Rivers surround this plain. The western alluvial plain is the Grand Prairie. It lies between the White River and the Arkansas River. Most of Arkansas' crops grow on the alluvial plain.

The West Gulf Coastal Plain covers southwestern Arkansas. This area of low land stretches from Arkansas to the Gulf of Mexico. Pine forests cover much of the coastal plain in Arkansas. Oil lies underground there.

Arkansas' lowest point is on the West Gulf Coastal Plain. Land at the Ouachita River near Arkansas' southern border is 55 feet (17 meters) above sea level. Sea level is the average surface level of the world's oceans.

Arkansas' Highlands

Arkansas has two highland areas. The Ouachita Mountains stand north of the West Gulf Coastal Plain. The Ozark Plateau covers northwestern Arkansas.

The Ouachita Mountains cover western Arkansas and part of Oklahoma. The Ouachita National Forest covers much of those mountains. The Ouachita River begins in the Ouachita Mountains. Lake Ouachita, Lake Hamilton, and Lake Catherine lie on the river.

The Ozark Plateau is home to the Ozark National Forest. The Boston Mountains rise along the plateau's southern edge. The Buffalo River and the White River begin in the northern Ozarks. Beaver Lake, Bull Shoals Lake, and Norfolk Lake lie along the White River.

The Arkansas Valley lies between the Ouachita Mountains and the Ozark Plateau. The Arkansas River flows east through the valley. Arkansas' highest point is in some mountains that rise up from the valley. Magazine Mountain stands 2,753 feet (839 meters) above sea level.

Climate

Arkansas has a warm climate. Summer temperatures in Arkansas range from 72 to 92 degrees Fahrenheit (22 to 33 degrees Celsius). Summers are hottest in southeastern Arkansas.

Shores Lake is one of many lakes that lie in the Ozarks.

Arkansas winters are usually mild. Winter temperatures range from 29 to 49 degrees Fahrenheit (-2 to 9 degrees Celsius). Winters are coldest in northern Arkansas.

Arkansas receives an average of 72 inches (183 centimeters) of rain each year. The Ouachita Mountains receive the most rain. Arkansas receives about six inches (15 centimeters) of snow each year. Most of the snow falls in the Ozarks.

Chapter 3
The People

Arkansas has the 33rd-largest population among the 50 states. Arkansas' population grew by 5.7 percent between 1990 and 1995. Many new Arkansans found jobs in the state's growing companies. Others retired in Arkansas' Ozarks.

About 53 percent of Arkansans live in or near cities. Arkansas' largest urban area includes Little Rock, Pine Bluff, and Hot Springs.

Arkansas' European Background
Arkansas' first European settlers were French soldiers and fur traders. They founded

About 53 percent of Arkansans live in urban areas such as Little Rock.

About 16 percent of Arkansans are African American.

Arkansas Post in 1686. This trading post stood near the Arkansas and Mississippi Rivers.

U.S. settlers moved to Arkansas during the early 1800s. Many of them had English, Scotch-Irish, and German backgrounds. Many of the settlers traveled from Missouri, Kentucky, and Tennessee. Others came from Georgia, Alabama, and Mississippi. They built plantations along Arkansas' rivers. They grew one main crop such as cotton on these large farms. The settlers founded Arkadelphia, Hot Springs, Little Rock, and Pine Bluff.

European settlers arrived in Arkansas in the late 1800s. Germans founded Stuttgart. Italians settled in Chicot and Benton counties. Today, about 83 percent of Arkansans have European backgrounds.

African Americans

Arkansas' first African Americans were slaves. French people brought them to North America during the early 1700s. U.S. settlers from southern states brought more slaves. They worked on plantations in Arkansas. By 1860, about 111,000 slaves lived in Arkansas. African Americans gained their freedom after the Civil War (1861–1865).

Today, about 16 percent of Arkansans are African American. Many African Americans farm on the Arkansas Delta. Others work in big cities such as Little Rock and Pine Bluff.

Hispanic Americans and Asian Americans

About 26,000 Hispanic Americans live in Arkansas. This is about 1 percent of the state's population. Arkansas' largest Hispanic groups have Mexican or Puerto Rican backgrounds. Many Hispanic Americans live in Fort Smith or Little Rock.

Asian Americans make up less than 1 percent of Arkansas' population. More than 17,000 Asian Americans live there today. More Asian Americans are moving to Arkansas. Many Asian families came from Laos and Vietnam. Others came from China, India, Japan, Korea, and the Philippines. Most Asian Americans in Arkansas live in urban areas.

Native Americans

Many Native American groups once lived in Arkansas. The groups included the Quapaw, Caddo, Osage, and Cherokee. By 1840, the U.S. government had moved these groups to Indian Territory in the area that is now Oklahoma.

About 26,000 Hispanic Americans live in Arkansas.

Today, about 15,000 Native Americans live in Arkansas. This is less than 1 percent of the population. There are no organized Native American tribes in Arkansas. Cherokee people make up the largest group of Native Americans living in Arkansas today. Most Cherokee people live in northwestern Arkansas.

Chapter 4
Arkansas History

The first people arrived in Arkansas about 12,000 years ago. By the 1500s, Osage and Caddo people lived there. By the 1600s, Quapaw people lived along the Arkansas River.

Spanish explorer Hernando de Soto led the first European exploration in Arkansas. His group reached what is now Arkansas in 1541. French explorer Henri de Tonti founded Arkansas Post in 1686. This was the first permanent European settlement in what is now Arkansas.

French explorer Henri de Tonti founded Arkansas Post in 1686.

People built cotton plantations along the Mississippi River.

Louisiana Purchase

In 1783, the United States claimed land east of the Mississippi River. The United States also wanted land west of the Mississippi River. In 1803, the United States bought that land from France in the Louisiana Purchase. The area that is now Arkansas was part of this land.

By 1819, about 14,000 U.S. settlers had moved to Arkansas. Some settlers from Southern states brought slaves. The slaves did much of the work on farms and plantations.

Statehood and Growth

Arkansas became the 25th state on June 15, 1836. Little Rock became the state capital.

Arkansas' businesses grew in the 1850s. Arkansans mined lead, iron, and coal. Lumber mills opened in the state's forests. People built cotton plantations along the Mississippi River. Plantation owners had many slaves to do their farm work.

Civil War and Reconstruction

Slavery divided the nation during the 1800s. Slavery was illegal in Northern states. Southerners feared that Congress would make laws against slavery in the South.

In February 1861, several Southern states withdrew from the United States. They formed a new nation called the Confederate States of America. Arkansas joined this new nation after the Civil War began.

The Civil War began in April 1861. Several battles took place in Arkansas. The United States won the Battle of Pea Ridge in March 1862. Later that year, the Confederate States won the Battle of Prairie Grove. The war ended in 1865 when the Confederate States of America surrendered.

The Southern states had to change their laws before rejoining the United States. This period was called Reconstruction. Arkansas passed laws that freed slaves. Other laws gave African American men the right to vote. Arkansas had to agree with laws that Congress set. Congress readmitted Arkansas to the United States in 1868.

Arkansas' landowners divided their plantations into smaller farms after slavery ended. Many former slaves and poor white people became tenant farmers. They worked land owned by other people and paid rent to owners with crops.

World Wars and Depression
The United States entered World War I (1914–1918) in 1917. The U.S. government built Camp Pike near Little Rock. The government stationed about 100,000 soldiers at the base. About 72,000 soldiers from Arkansas helped win the war.

Floods in the 1920s ruined farm fields in Arkansas.

The 1920s were hard times in Arkansas. The price of cotton fell. Floods ruined farm fields. Then the Great Depression (1929–1939) hit the nation. Many Arkansans lost their land during this time. Thousands of people left the state.

In 1941, the United States entered World War II (1939–1945). Arkansas' aluminum and oil companies hired more workers. The companies provided metal and fuel for military equipment.

The End of Segregation

Schools and other public places in the South were segregated until 1954. In 1954, the U.S. Supreme Court ruled against separate public schools. Arkansas did not follow this ruling right away. African American students and white students still attended separate public schools.

Nine African Americans tried to attend Little Rock's Central High School in 1957. Only white students attended Central High School. Some white Arkansans made it impossible for the African American students to enter. President Dwight Eisenhower sent U.S. troops to help the African American students enter the school.

Many other Arkansans worked to stop segregation. By the 1970s, most Arkansas public schools were open to all students.

Recent Challenges

Since the 1960s, more businesses have come to Arkansas. But logging companies and poultry plants have polluted Arkansas' land and rivers. Farmers raise poultry such as chickens and

U.S. troops helped African American students enter Little Rock's Central High School.

turkeys for their eggs and meat. Many Arkansans are working to stop pollution.

Arkansans also are trying to improve training for their workers. In 1997, the state passed the Workforce Education Act. Under this act, workers learn the skills needed for higher-paying jobs. A skilled workforce may help attract new companies to Arkansas.

Chapter 5
Arkansas Business

Service businesses are Arkansas' most
valuable businesses. Manufacturing
is Arkansas' largest business. Other important
Arkansas businesses are farming, logging,
and mining.

Service Businesses

Trade is Arkansas' main service business. Trade
businesses buy and sell goods. Wal-Mart's
headquarters are in Bentonville. Wal-Mart is the
world's largest retailer. A retailer sells goods to
the public.

Many Arkansans work for the government.
Some have jobs at Little Rock Air Force
Base. Some have offices in the state capitol.

**Many Arkansans work for the government. Some have
offices in the state capitol.**

Tourism is an important service business. Tourists spend about $3 billion in Arkansas each year. Hotels, resorts, and museums receive much of this money.

Manufacturing

About one-fourth of Arkansas' workers have manufacturing jobs. Packaged foods are Arkansas' leading manufactured goods. Tyson Foods is the world's largest poultry packaging company. Its headquarters are in Springdale.

Arkansas' paper mills make cardboard and paper. Some Arkansas factories manufacture furniture, electric motors, and automobile parts.

Farming

Arkansas' crops are important to the nation. Arkansas produces more rice than any other U.S. state. Soybeans are Arkansas' most valuable crop. Cotton and wheat are other important crops.

Arkansas raises the most broilers in the United States. The young chickens are raised for their meat. Farmers in northwestern Arkansas raise more than 1 million broilers per year.

Logging is an important business in Arkansas.

Logging and Mining

Logging is another important business in Arkansas. Loggers cut down oak and hickory trees in Arkansas' highland forests. They harvest pine trees in southwestern Arkansas.

Arkansas' top three mining products are oil, natural gas, and bromine. About one-half of the world's bromine comes from Arkansas. Manufacturers use bromine to make fuels, dyes, and fire extinguishers. Arkansas also leads the United States in the production of bauxite. Manufacturers use bauxite to make aluminum.

Chapter 6
Seeing the Sights

Visitors to Arkansas enjoy the state's rivers, mountains, and springs. Many towns host music, craft, and food festivals. Museum displays show the state's history.

Little Rock Area

Little Rock is near the center of Arkansas. It is the state capital. Quapaw Quarter in downtown Little Rock is the oldest section of the city. Visitors tour homes built there during the late 1800s.

Pinnacle Mountain State Park is northwest of Little Rock. Visitors hike on trails there. Park workers teach visitors about the environment.

Visitors to Quapaw Quarter tour homes from the 1800s.

Visitors tour President Bill Clinton's first home in Hope.

Toltec Mounds State Park is southeast of Little Rock. Native Americans built mounds there about 1,400 years ago. These huge mounds are the tallest mounds in the state.

Southwestern Arkansas Highlights

Hot Springs is the largest city in southwestern Arkansas. It is home to Hot Springs National Park. About 1 million gallons (3.8 million liters) of hot water flow from the park's 47 springs each day. Pipes carry the water to bathhouses. Visitors can bathe in some of them.

Hope is southwest of Hot Springs. President Bill Clinton was born in Hope. Visitors tour his first home. Hope also is known for its giant watermelons. The town hosts the Watermelon Festival each August. The grower of the largest watermelon wins a prize.

Eastern Arkansas Highlights

Lake Chicot is in southeastern Arkansas. Visitors camp and fish on Arkansas' biggest natural lake. Bird watchers observe many different kinds of birds at Lake Chicot State Park.

Helena is on the Mississippi River. Helena hosts the King Biscuit Blues Festival each October. Blues is a style of slow, sad music first sung by African Americans. This music started on the Mississippi River Delta in the late 1800s.

West Memphis lies farther north along the Mississippi River Delta. Visitors tour nearby cotton, soybean, and catfish farms. Blues musicians play music during some tours.

Ozark Highlights

Many towns in the Ozarks are famous for cold-water springs. Mammoth Spring is in the northeastern Ozarks. Eureka Springs is in the northwestern Ozarks. Cold water bubbles in pools from the town's 60 springs.

Mountain View is southwest of Mammoth Spring. This town is home to the Ozark Folk Center. Crafters show visitors how to make quilts, candles, and baskets. The Folk Center also hosts the Arkansas State Old-time Fiddle Championship each September.

Fayetteville is southwest of Eureka Springs. Fayetteville is the Ozarks' largest city. It is home to the University of Arkansas. The school's sports teams are the Razorbacks.

Western Arkansas River Valley Towns

Fort Smith is south of Fayetteville. It stands at the Arkansas-Oklahoma border. Fort Smith is Arkansas' second-largest city. The city holds the Old Fort Days Rodeo each May. Thousands of people bring horses from throughout the United States and Canada.

Alma is northeast of Fort Smith. Alma is the Spinach Captial of the World. Workers pack the Popeye brand of spinach there. A statue of Popeye stands downtown.

Morrilton is farther east. The Museum of Automobiles is there. The museum displays historical cars dating back to 1904.

Arkansas Time Line

10,000 B.C. — The first people reach what is now Arkansas.

A.D. 1500 — Osage and Caddo people are in the area that is now Arkansas.

1541 — Spanish explorer Hernando de Soto enters what is now Arkansas.

1600s — Quapaw people settle along the Arkansas River.

1686 — Henry de Tonti founds Arkansas Post. It is the area's first European settlement.

1700s — Cherokee people settle in the Ozarks.

1803 — The United States purchases the land that is now Arkansas from France in the Louisiana Purchase.

1807–1819 — Settlers found Hot Springs, Little Rock, and Fort Smith.

1828 — The U.S. government removes Arkansas Cherokees to Indian Territory.

1830s–1840 — The U.S. government removes the rest of Arkansas' Native Americans to Indian Territory.

1836 — Arkansas becomes the 25th state.

1838–1839 — The U.S. government removes Native American tribes from the eastern

United States to Indian territory. They travel through Arkansas on the Trail of Tears.

1861 — The Civil War begins; Arkansas leaves the United States and joins the Confederate States of America.

1865 — The Civil War ends when the Confederate States of America surrenders.

1868 — Congress allows Arkansas to rejoin the United States.

1906 — John M. Huddleston finds diamonds near Murfreesboro.

1932 — Hattie Caraway of Arkansas is the first woman elected to the U.S. Senate.

1948 — Arkansas is the first southern state to integrate its public universities.

1957 — African American students enter Little Rock's Central High School with the help of U.S. troops.

1983 — Arkansas becomes the first state to require teachers to pass a basic skills test.

1992 — Arkansas native Bill Clinton is elected the 42nd president of the United States.

1994 — The University of Arkansas basketball team wins the NCAA championship.

1997 — Tornadoes kill 25 people in Arkansas.

Famous Arkansans

Maya Angelou (1928–) Poet and author who wrote *I Know Why the Caged Bird Sings,* which describes her youth in Arkansas; grew up in Stamps.

Daisy Gatson Bates (1922–) Civil rights leader and newspaper owner who helped integrate Little Rock's Central High School; born in Huttig.

William Jefferson (Bill) Clinton (1946–) Politician who served as Arkansas' governor (1979–1981, 1983–1993) and as president of the United States (1993–); born in Hope.

Jocelyn Elders (1933–) Doctor who served as surgeon general of the United States (1993–1994); born in Schaal.

John H. Johnson (1918–) Publisher who founded *Negro Digest*, *Jet*, and *Ebony* magazines; received Presidential Medal of Freedom; born in Arkansas City.

Douglas MacArthur (1880–1964) Military leader who served as a general in the U.S. Army in World War I, World War II, and the Korean War (1950–1953); born in Little Rock.

Scottie Pippen (1965–) Star basketball player for the University of Central Arkansas who now plays for the Chicago Bulls; born in Hamburg.

Sarasen (1735?–1832) Arkansas' last Quapaw chief; helped American settlers in Arkansas; buried in Pine Bluff.

Mary Steenburgen (1953–) Actress who won an Academy Award as best supporting actress (1980) for her role in *Melvin and Howard*; born in Newport.

Louise McPhetridge Thaden (1906–1979) Pioneer aviator who won the first Women's Air Derby in 1929; grew up in Bentonville.

Words to Know

alluvial plain (uh-LOO-vee-uhl PLANE)—an area of rich soil created by flooding rivers

bauxite (BAWK-site)—a mineral used to make aluminum

blues (BLOOZ)—a style of slow, sad music first sung by African Americans

broiler (BROI-lur)—a young chicken raised for its meat

bromine (BROH-meen)—a chemical used to make fuels, dyes, and fire extinguishers

oxbow lake (OKS-boh LAKE)—a U-shaped lake formed when a river changes course

plantation (plan-TAY-shuhn)—a large farm where one main crop is grown

Reconstruction (ree-kuhn-STRUHK-shuhn)— the period after the Civil War when the Southern states reorganized their governments

tenant farmer (TEN-uhnt FARM-uhr)—a person who works land owned by someone else and pays rent with crops

To Learn More

Aylesworth, Thomas G. and Virginia L. Aylesworth. *South Central: Arkansas, Kansas, Louisiana, Missouri, Oklahoma.* State Studies. New York: Chelsea House, 1995.

Di Piazza, Domenica. *Arkansas.* Hello U.S.A. Minneapolis: Lerner Publications, 1994.

Fradin, Dennis Brindell. *Arkansas.* From Sea to Shining Sea. Chicago: Children's Press, 1994.

O'Neill, Laurie A. *Little Rock: The Desegregation of Central High.* Spotlight on American History. Brookfield, Conn.: Millbrook Press, 1994.

Thompson, Kathleen. *Arkansas.* Portrait of America. Austin, Texas: Raintree Steck-Vaughn, 1996.

Internet Sites

Arkansas—The Natural State
http://www.arkansas.com

Excite Travel: Arkansas, United States
http://www.city.net/countries/united_states/
arkansas

Hot Springs National Park
http://www.nps.gov/hosp

TRAVEL.org—Arkansas
http://travel.org/arkansas.html

Welcome to the State of Arkansas
http://www.state.ar.us

Useful Addresses

Arkansas Department of Parks and Tourism
One Capitol Mall
Little Rock, AR 72201

Crater of Diamonds State Park
Route 1, Box 364
Murfreesboro, AR 71958

Hot Springs National Park
Superintendent
P.O. Box 1860
Hot Springs, AR 71902-1860

Quapaw Quarter Historic Neighborhoods
P.O. Box 165023
Little Rock, AR 72216

William Clinton Birthplace/Boyhood Homes
Hope Visitor Center and Museum
South Main and Division Streets
Hope, AR 71801

Index